BACKYARD COMPOSTING

John Roulac

Green Earth Books

This revised edition published in the UK in 1999
by Green Earth Books, an imprint of Green Books,
Foxhole, Dartington, Totnes, Devon TQ9 6EB.

Reprinted 1999, 2000 (four times), 2001

First published in the USA in 1992 by
Harmonious Technologies, P.O. Box 1716, Sebastopol, California 95473.

Author: John W. Roulac
Editor: Marialyce Pedersen
Editor of UK edition: Nicky Scott
Cover picture: Bob Gale
Printed & bound in Great Britain
by J. W. Arrowsmith Ltd, Bristol

ISBN 1 900322 11 0

The information contained in this book is true and complete
to the best of our knowledge. However, no guarantees are placed on the
results. The responsibilities lie with the reader.

Acknowledgments

*The following people provided invaluable technical review
for the original US edition:*

Dr. Tony Dominski, education director,
Community Environmental Council

Dr. Clark Gregory, "Compost Man"

Richard Kashmanian, senior economist,
U.S. Environmental Protection Agency

Matthew Werner, soil ecologist,
Agroecology Program, UC Santa Cruz

Ruth Richardson, master composter,
Recycling Council of Ontario

Jim McNelly, president,
McNelly Group

Dr. Bill Roley, director,
Permaculture Institute of Southern California

Any philosophical conclusions are the
sole responsibility of Harmonious Technologies.

Harmonious Technologies would like to thank everyone
who provided inspiration and assistance in the creation of
this book, including:

Isabel Adams
Lynne Blackman
Bruce Braunstein
Brenda Burglas
Peter Dukich
Taryn Henry
Jeff Hunts
Hari Khalsa

Jerry Moles
Bill Mollison
Sonia Nordenson
John Perlin
Dan Poynter
Stephan Reeve
Julia Russell

Don Sexton
George Stevens
Robert W. Tansill
Carl & Nan Tolbert
Mark Walsh
Bob Walters
Howard Westley
Steven Zien

and for the UK edition:

Pauline Pears of the Henry Doubleday Research Association
George Sobol, Patsy Garrard and Jamie Saunders of the UK Permaculture
Association, Andy Langford, Pete Riley of Save Waste and Prosper, Lewis
Herbert of Essex County Council, Dave Middlemass, The Community
Composting Network, Patrick Whitefield, and Plants for a Future.

Table of Contents

Introduction

The Earth has been having a tough time lately, due to such conditions as overflowing landfills, loss of rainforests, air pollution, chemical poisoning, soil erosion and disappearing ozone layer.

Much of this is the result of how we live. Thinking about or implementing change on a national or global basis can be overwhelming. Composting allows you to do something for the part of the Earth you live with day by day: your own garden.

Home composting is probably the single most effective action you can personally take to help the planet: you will lighten your dustbin (incidentally removing the smelliest fraction); stop polluting - and unhealthy - bonfires; reduce the need to water your garden; increase your plant growth and health, by replacing the need to use polluting and toxic chemical fertilisers and pesticides. And you can use your compost and leaf mould in potting mixtures, replacing the need to use peat from fast-disappearing peat bogs. Trees, earthworms, butterflies and other flora and fauna will be thankful for your composting achievements.

Best of luck in your composting adventures!

John Roulac and the staff of
Harmonious Technologies

A Crash Course in Composting

Composting is like cooking, with many recipes and variations. Here is the basic approach:

All composting "ingredients" generally fall under one of two categories: "browns" or "greens." Browns are dry, hard materials such as wood chips, dried leaves and other plants. Greens are fresh, soft, moist materials such as grass cuttings and food scraps (avoid meats, fats and grease, as these attract rats and flies - see Worm Bins, page 52).

1. Collect as many browns and greens as you can to start your compost pile. Larger piles tend to hold moisture better and decompose faster.

2. Place approximately equal amounts of browns and greens in a heap or bin. Always cover food scraps with other composting materials.

3. Soak well with water to create uniform dampness (damp as a wrung-out sponge). Cover pile with an old carpet (preferably natural fibre of wool, flax or hemp), or cardboard or plastic to keep moisture in and prevent oversoaking from rain.

For quicker composting (1-3 months):
- Chop materials into smaller pieces and moisten.
- Alternate 3" to 6" layers of greens and browns.
- Mix the pile by turning and stirring.
- Make sure the heap remains moist.

For slower composting (3-6 months plus):
- Just keep adding materials to the pile or bin and sprinkling it with water. It's that simple!

Troubleshooting:
- Odours? Turn and add brown materials.
- Dry pile? Add water, greens and mix.
- Fruit flies? Stir and add leaves or grass.

– See page 35 for hot composting recipes

Composting Questions & Answers

What is composting?

Composting is the natural process of decomposition and recycling of organic material into a humus-rich soil amendment known as compost.

Is composting considered recycling?

Yes. Composting is nature's way of recycling. The Government includes composting in its definitions of recycling.

Are garden clippings waste?

No. Just as a glass bottle is a valuable resource, so is a pile of garden clippings. Glass is scrap material waiting to be melted and reformed, while leaves, grass, food scraps, and paper towels are organic materials waiting to be converted into compost.

How much material is already home-composted in Britain?

Over 400,000 tonnes a year!

What percentage of the household refuse in the UK is made up of garden clippings and kitchen scraps?

Approximately 30%.

Why shouldn't organic materials go to the landfill?

In a landfill, organic matter reacts with other materials and creates toxic leachate that may contaminate nearby streams or groundwater. Organic matter placed in airtight landfills stops the earth's natural cycle of decomposition. This cycle plays a crucial role in the health of our environment. The airless (anaerobic) conditions mean that instead of composting the materials ferment, giving off methane - an explosive, potent contributor to the greenhouse

effect. Furthermore, the site is unstable and liable to subsidence.

How does compost benefit the soil?

Compost improves soil structure, texture and aeration and increases its water-holding capacity. It loosens clay soils and helps sandy soils retain water. Adding compost to soils aids in erosion control, promotes soil fertility and stimulates healthy root development in plants. Plants grown in compost-rich soils are stronger and more resistant to disease and pests. Research carried out by Eco-Sci of Exeter has proved that compost-grown plants are resistant to red-core in strawberries, club-root in brassicas, white rot in onions, blight in peas, and take-all and foot rot in cereals. See reference to compost tea on p58.

Roman Statesman Advocated Composting

The Roman statesman Marcus Cato introduced composting as a way to build soil fertility throughout the Roman Empire more than 2,000 years ago. A scientist and farmer, Cato believed in the use of compost as a primary soil builder. He considered compost production and use essential for maintaining healthy agricultural soils. Cato insisted that all raw materials such as animal manures and vegetation be composted before being ploughed into the soil.

Can compost replace petroleum-based fertilizers?

Yes. Generous amounts of rich compost can supply the nutrients needed for healthy plant growth. In addition, planting green cover crops such as clover or vetch can significantly boost nitrogen levels in the soil.

Do I need a bin to make compost?

No. Compost can be made in open piles. However, bins help keep piles neat, retain heat and moisture and are appropriate for many urban situations.

What does ready-to-use compost look like?

Compost is dark brown or black, crumbly, humus-rich topsoil with a sweet aroma of good earth.

How long does it take to produce compost?

The composting process can take as little as one month or as long as 12 to 24 months. Factors include techniques used, moisture levels, the balance of brown and green materials, and seasonal temperatures.

What role does the ratio of browns and greens play in decomposition?

By having a balance of wet, green materials (grass clippings, food scraps, manures) and dry, brown materials (dry leaves and woody materials), compost piles generate high temperatures that slowly "simmer" and create compost. Using only brown materials in the pile will slow down the composting process because piles do not generate sufficient heat. And, by adding only wet, green materials without dry, brown bulking agents like leaves, odours may develop.

What role does moisture content play in decomposition?

Moisture is often overlooked and plays a key role in composting. Keeping your pile moist will provide a friendly and safe environment for microorganisms (bacteria and fungi) that assist in the process of decomposition.

Should compost piles be covered?

In hotter climates, a cover will retain a compost pile's moisture. Plastic, wood chips or straw can be used. Covering helps to keep piles moist in summer and prevents them from getting too soggy in the rain or snow.

Does the compost pile have a smell?

Fresh compost has a pleasant aroma. Foul odours occur only where there is a lack of oxygen or when there is too much wet, green material and too little brown material. Odours can be alleviated by turning or poking the pile and mixing green and brown materials together.

What is mulch?

Mulch is any material (such as wood chips, paper, or rocks) placed over the soil to reduce evaporation and erosion, prevent weed growth, and insulate plants from extreme temperature changes.

What's the difference between compost and mulch?

Compost is a ready-to-use soil enricher that looks and feels like dark, crumbly soil. Mulch is any material used to cover soil in order to retain moisture and suppress weeds. Shredded garden clippings make an excellent mulch. Compost can also be used as a mulch.

How much time is needed to compost?

A low-maintenance composting recycler's approach will require as little as five minutes per week, which is less time than it takes to bag leaves or clippings, tie them and take them to the kerb. A composting connoisseur may spend 10 to 15 minutes a week, and will produce compost faster and of finer texture.

1   *Compost Happens*

W E CAN OBSERVE the process of composting by walking through a lush forest and scooping up a layer of fallen leaves under a huge tree. The top layers are recognizable as leaves, twigs and needles. But below these are last season's leaves, which have been transformed into rich, crumbly soil. We call this process decomposition, and it has been occurring for millions of years.

As we explore composting further, remember that compost unfailingly happens, just as the leaves from the forest floor are always changing from one form to another.

We can visit the forest ten or twenty years later and the same huge tree under which we stood has now fallen and been converted into a home for billions of microorganisms, earthworms and insects. These little creatures have done such a good job, along with the heat of the sun, water from the clouds and oxygen from the living forest, that a beautiful young seedling is now proudly growing from the rich, crumbly soil in the middle of the old tree.

Compost happens, naturally, whether it is in the forest or in your own backyard. The more we understand this dynamic process, the better off our gardens and communities will be.

Do You Need a Ph.D. to Compost?

There are hundreds of well-written journals and books on the science of modern composting. One could spend a lifetime learning the intricacies of the lives of psychrophiles, actinomycetes and bacteria.

For now, let's just realize that these friendly micro-organisms naturally like to eat leaves, grass, manures, food scraps, paper towels and other organic materials. When you start a compost bin in your garden, they, along with worms and insects, are your team of volunteers. They need air, water and food materials to sustain their functions. Provide a friendly "eco home" in your compost pile and nature will do the rest. There is no need to import them – they are already there naturally.

Healthy Plant Food

We can think of compost pile microorganisms as liberators of the nutrients which make plants grow strong and healthy. The nutrients they release are so wonderful and so ideally adapted to plants' needs that they are a far better soil enricher than human-engineered fertilizers. That's why we say "compost feeds the soil." The Earth's forests, which rely on decaying matter and nitrogen-fixing plants for their soil fertility, have been producing lush and fertile plant growth for millions of years without the help of any petroleum-based fertilizers.

Soil needs what compost's life processes give: nutrients that release their nutrition gradually and in small doses over long periods of time.

Synthetic fertilizers provide quick jolts of nutrition to the plant roots, but in the process they stymie root develop-ment, while compost-enriched soils encourage healthy and abundant root development. Without the life process that distinguishes composted soil from soil fertilized with synthetic ingredients, the skin of our planet will quickly degenerate into an inert, barren landscape.

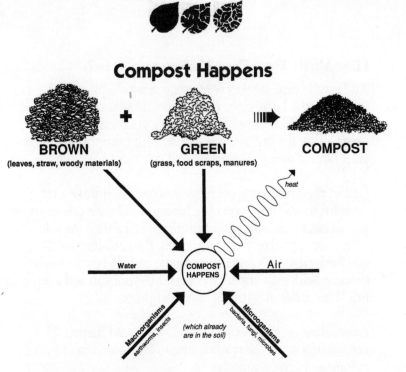

Compost Happens

BROWN
(leaves, straw, woody materials)

+

GREEN
(grass, food scraps, manures)

COMPOST

heat

Water → **COMPOST HAPPENS** ← Air

Macroorganisms
earthworms, insects

(which already are in the soil)

Microorganisms
bacteria, fungi, microbes

Cover the heap with: Plastic sheet; Carpet; Cardboard etc.

alternate layers high in Nitrogen, eg grass, manure; sappy weeds

with layers high in Carbon eg: Dry Stalks; Shredded woody materials + paper; Straw

thoroughly soak dry materials

Nettles, seaweed urine; fresh manure & ½ finished compost make good activators

A heap made in one go from pre-assembled materials will rapidly heat up, especially if contained in a well-insulated box, using a mixture of fresh sappy materials high in nitrogen, and plenty of well-soaked tougher materials high in carbon. You need a good mass to get the heap heating up - at least a cubic metre, more is better. All you need to do is bring the right ingredients together, and compost happens!

How Much Time Does Composting Take?

Add up the time it takes you to bag grass clippings and leaves, tie the bags, place them in dustbins and drag them to the kerb. Now, instead of bagging your garden clippings, place the organic portion on your compost pile or in your bin – a simple enclosure is all you need.

Rather than returning every week to manhandle several dustbins to the kerb, you only have to tend your pile every few weeks or months. You can stir, poke or turn the pile with your shovel or pitchfork, check the moisture levels, add fresh materials and your organic materials will slowly simmer, with little more attention. Fill your bin and keep it full. The material "shrinks" as it composts.

Depending on the method you choose (see Chapter 4), your compost will be ready to use in less than a month, or as long as 12 to 24 months.

Some dedicated compost connoisseurs return every few days to add more materials to the pile and perhaps say a few compost words or prayers!

You can also use food scraps (except meat), paper towels and toilet paper tubes for composting. Store them in a bucket or food container with a tight-fitting lid and then add them to the compost pile.

If you are only composting garden clippings, you could spend as little as five minutes a week maintaining your compost pile. If you are composting kitchen scraps, figure in a few additional minutes. Remember, spending just a few minutes a week composting will transform your rubbish into treasure.

Mixing the Batch

The difference between a beginner and an experienced composter is quite simple. The beginner is aware of fewer pointers for making compost. The veteran intentionally takes the time to provide a friendly environment for the various elements – see the "Compost Happens" diagram.

There are as many different recipes for baking a fine-tasting casserole as there are cooks. The same is true in making a batch of compost. An experienced composter may create compost a little more easily than a beginner. Yet both will make usable, soil-enriching compost. Each time you make a new batch, you will refine your skills further.

Difficult Materials

Even some of the most dedicated compost makers find they have materials they cannot compost easily. Burning woody materials provides a small amount of potash, but bonfires are a nuisance to neighbours, extremely hazardous to health, and polluting. It is far better to come up with alternatives. The simplest is just to make as compact a heap as you can. This will become a wildlife refuge for all manner of insects, wood-boring beetles, frogs, toads, newts and other useful pest controllers. Some gardeners 'weave' woody material into a kind of hedge which is not only a wildlife reserve, but also a wind break. Or you can make a German Mound Garden, which uses a core of woody materials two spits (spade-depths) deep, covered with layers of progressively softer or more composted material. These mounds are capped off with the earth excavated to accommodate the woody core and planted up in the first year with shallow rooting plants or peas and beans, which provide their own nitrogen.

There is no way to fail with composting. It just may take a little longer, because – ultimately – compost happens.

2   *Soil Fertility*

I NTERACTION BETWEEN CIVILIZATION and the Earth's
natural resources has taken many forms throughout
history. A conservation-based society understands that a
healthy, diverse and vibrant ecosystem is beneficial for its
members.

Five thousand years ago, in what is known as the Fertile
Crescent, the great Mesopotamian civilization thrived in
the lush Tigris/Euphrates River Valley, considered to be
the birthplace of Western Civilization. The people of this
region invented the wheel and recorded, on clay tablets, the
first written set of laws. They also developed and cultivated
several important modern-day crops, including dates, figs,
mulberries and pistachios.

According to John Perlin's classic book, *A Forest Journey*,
"The ruler at that time, Gilgamesh, wished to make a name
for himself by building up his city ... fortunately for
Gilgamesh, a great primeval forest lay before him.

"That such vast tracts of timber grew near Southern
Mesopotamia might seem a flight of fancy, considering the
present barren condition of the land, but before the intru-
sion of civilizations an almost unbroken forest flourished in
the hills and mountains surrounding the Fertile Crescent
... Gilgamesh's war against the forest has been repeated for
generations, in every corner of the globe, in order to supply
building and fuel stocks needed for each civilization's
continual material growth."

*An ancient bas relief depicts
a forest scene in the Near East.*

Later, the Roman Christian and Arab Muslim empires placed great demands on native forests, harvesting wood for ship building. Then they permitted their herds to overgraze on newly deforested lands. The great cedar forests of Lebanon were gradually stripped, as were the dense stands of the Sahara Forest in Northern Africa, which we now know as the Sahara Desert. These civilizations moved northward through Greece, Italy and Europe, laying waste to the forests before them.

North America

In the rich land called North America, two separate ways of treating the Earth came face to face. New settlers began "taming" the wilderness to serve them as fields for the animals and crops they wished to raise. Native Americans looked in sorrow at the lack of respect for nature the newcomers exhibited.

In the words of Lakota Chief Luther Standing Bear, "The Lakota was a true naturist – a lover of nature. He loved the Earth and all things of the Earth, the attachment growing with age. The old people came literally to love the soil and they sat or reclined on the ground with a feeling of being close to a mothering power. It was good for the skin to touch the Earth and the old people liked to remove their moccasins and walk with bare feet on the sacred Earth ... it was the final abiding place of all things that lived and grew. The soil was soothing, strengthening, cleansing and healing."

Two early founders of America, George Washington and Thomas Jefferson, were strong advocates of crop rotation, composting and other methods of ensuring continuing healthy soils.

Yet today America is losing over three billion tons of topsoil a year, with as much as 700 million tons washing into the Gulf of Mexico alone. Perhaps it's time now to heed the words of President Franklin Roosevelt: "The nation that destroys its soil destroys itself."

In the Dust Bowl days of the 1930s, President Roosevelt signed legislation that helped create more than 3,000 local soil and water conservation districts whose job it is to prevent soil erosion.

The Fertility of Our Future

History shows us that erosion and drought follow deforestation, overgrazing and broad-scale destructive ploughing. It is evident that maintaining healthy trees and using compost and mulch are good for our own landscapes as well as for farms, forests and fields.

Prince Charles, during a presentation at the Sixth National Conference on Organic Food Production, said, "There is no doubt that over the last few years a growing anxiety has developed among all sections of the community of the consequences of modern intensive farming methods. It is increasingly felt by members of the public that large-scale soil erosion, the destruction of wildlife habitat and the excessive use of chemicals … cannot continue unabated without ruining the countryside."

If our current cycle of deforestation and drought continues unchecked, many biologists and scientists believe that much of the world's remaining forests and productive lands will disappear in the early part of the 21st century. With the soil will go the Earth's plants, animals and perhaps human beings. Losing our productive lands may cause humans to be considered an "endangered species."

Why Compost?

Compost can save you money:

- ❧ Reduces waste
- ❧ Provides free soil amendment
- ❧ Retains soil moisture – save on water bills

Compost can help your garden:

- ❧ Feeds the soil
- ❧ Prevents soil erosion
- ❧ Improves yields of fruits, vegetables, flowers and herbs

Composting can improve our environment:

- ❧ Turns waste into a valuable resource
- ❧ Saves limited landfill space
- ❧ Recycles nutrients back into the soil

Personal Action Makes a Difference

Thinking of the problems we face can be overwhelming. Yet changes do take root when individuals take action in their own lives. In recent years, many people have started to recycle. Instead of being throwaway items, bottles, cans and paper are now valuable resources.

Garden clippings were also once considered rubbish or waste. Today, millions of people are making soil in their gardens via composting. Perhaps the single most powerful thing we can do as stewards of the planet is to care for the small patches of land surrounding our homes. A vibrant, living soil, after all, forms the foundation for our life needs: food, oxygen and water. Remember, compost feeds the soil and the soil feeds us! By composting, we reap the benefits – a more beautiful garden and a reduction in water and fertilizer bills.

More than that, though, composters can take pride in having lessened society's search for more holes in the ground to fill with rubbish.

3   *Let's Start at Home*

OMPOSTERS ARE RECYCLERS, and millions of recyclers are now adding composting to their recycling activities.

Personal Goals in Composting

It's a good idea to define your personal goals in composting. Are you a composting recycler whose purpose is to reduce your personal volume of stuff going to landfills, mass burn incinerators or sewer plants, with the added side benefit of returning organic matter back into the soil?

Or are you a composting connoisseur whose major objective is to produce plenty of fabulous nutrient-rich compost for your garden?

The compost connoisseur will often concentrate more on the fine points of composting while the compost recycler may pursue a low-maintenance, timesaving approach. Throughout this book, options for both composting categories are discussed.

Composting and the Four R's

Composting **reduces** your generation of rubbish. After you reduce its volume, you can **reuse** the compost in your yard. Then, the compost **recycles** nutrients back into soil and plant life. That's why the Government considers composting to be recycling. Increased plant growth helps to **restore** the health and beauty of our neighbourhoods.

Kids Love Composting

Today's generation of eco-conscious kids can be a big help in making compost happen at your home. A fun and educational job to assign young children is carrying the house bucket full of kitchen scraps outside to the compost bin. This activity brings the wonders of science and nature to life, as they see last week's leftovers becoming rich soil.

Landfills Are Filling Up

We are running out of places to bury our rubbish. In fact, in many communities landfills are filling up rapidly, and who wants to live near a landfill? It just makes sense to conserve our existing landfill capacity by reducing materials sent to such facilities, and by only landfilling inert material.

The European Landfill Directive's target (April 1999) is to reduce the amount of municipal waste going to landfill to 75% of the 1995 level by 2006 [2010 for the UK], to 50% by 2009 [2013], and to 35% by 2016 [2020]. Composting is the answer! Local authorities are devising a range of strategies to meet this target, with home composting high on the agenda. Composting removes the smelliest, most awkward fraction of the waste stream, making it easier to sort and reclaim the remainder. Next in importance in the 'waste hierarchy' is community composting and recycling. In Chapter 10 we will explore how innovative communities are offering help, and compost bins at low cost.

Slow the Flow and Save Some Dough

By keeping materials off the kerb and out of the landfill, you may even save some money through reduced refuse collection fees. Transporting leaves, grass, vegetation and food scraps in lorries and then processing them at a composting facility or landfill creates needless waste and costs money. It has been calculated that, for North America, if the majority of people composted, they could save one

hundred million dollars (around £60 million) annually in reduced refuse collection fees. Eco-Sci have calculated that hauling materials for composting more than five miles is uneconomic. They are working with local farmers to compost on the farm and use the compost there too!

You are also doing your personal part to reduce environmental problems, such as groundwater contamination and methane gas generation at landfills. Keeping food scraps out of the garbage disposal and composting them instead eases the load on sewage plants which empty into our rivers, lakes and oceans.

Choosing a Spot

Easy access to your kitchen, available water and enough space for temporary storage of organic materials are all helpful. Do not place your pile adjoining a wooden fence or building; otherwise, the wood will rot over time. Good drainage is important; settled water slows down the simmering process. Placing your pile on a concrete or paved surface is not encouraged, as this prevents soil microorganisms from doing their job.

In arid climates, an ideal location for a compost pile is under a tree. The shade prevents the pile from drying out too fast and allows it to receive adequate sunlight during the day. In cold regions, direct sunshine is recommended. It is better (but not essential) to avoid placing your pile under trees such as pine, eucalyptus, bay laurel, juniper, acacia, oleander, or black walnut, which produce acids that may inhibit plant growth.

Veteran composters often place their pile in a spot where they will plant the next year. This saves time and gives new plants added vigour. Just move the pile around your garden and watch how fertile your soil becomes!

Snow, Sleet or Rain

In winter, the composting process slows down significantly due to cold temperatures. One tip is to build a larger pile and/or cover it. Greater mass will retain more heat. If it rains heavily where you live, it's a good idea to put a cover or lid over your pile. Too much water will retard the rate of decomposition. Insulating your heap will help to keep it more active.

Airy or Airless?

There are two separate families of micro-organisms which can work and live in compost piles, distinguished by the presence or lack of oxygen. *Aerobic* micro-organisms are at work in open-air, oxygen-rich composting bins or piles, and *anaerobic* ones are found in closed-air bins or piles covered by plastic sheeting, which limit oxygen flow. Both break down organic matter well.

Of course, there will always be some oxygen in closed-air piles, coming through the soil itself and when opening the bin or removing the plastic sheeting to add materials. Compost scientists can debate for hours on the merits of aerobic or anaerobic composting, but for the backyard composter, the basic concept is all you need to know. Whichever system you choose, open or closed, be assured that the right micro-organisms will find your pile.

Tools of the Trade

Many composters use a long-handled pitchfork to easily build piles and to mix materials thoroughly. A tool called a compost turner or aerator may also be used to poke and aerate the pile. A compost thermometer, which has a long probe, will accurately measure how hot your pile is.

Do You Need a Container?

As was said in Chapter 1, compost happens, so a compost bin or barrel merely organizes your materials for you. Some people produce excellent compost without any container at all.

In a city setting, however, a container creates a neat and tidy structure that retains heat well, is visually pleasing and serves as a reminder for you to compost.

Please note that the listing of any particular composting product is in no way an endorsement by Harmonious Technologies. Our purpose is to give you a sampling of product options. Any decision to purchase a product is, of course, up to you.

Soil Incorporation

Soil incorporation involves simply burying kitchen scraps and other garden materials (other than meats, bones, fats

and other animal products which attract pests) in fallow areas of the garden or around drip lines of trees and shrubs. A hole or row about a foot deep is dug. Food scraps are then placed in the hole, chopped up and mixed into the soil, and covered with at least 8" of soil. The depth will prevent animals from digging materials up.

Heap Composting

Heap composting is a simple method whereby materials are piled on top of each other directly on the ground. Materials can be added immediately or stockpiled until enough are available to make a good-sized heap. A small pile (2'x 2') tends to remain at a lower temperature and the heating process will be hindered. A pile about 5 – 6' tall in the middle is ideal for rapid decomposition. Once the heap is large enough, you can build another one.

Heaps do tend to sprawl and shrink to short mounds. To organize your compost, consider a simple enclosure.

8 Feet

Compost in a Dustbin

Perhaps you have an extra plastic dustbin that you use to put leaves and grass in. To convert your dustbin into a composter, just cut off the bottom with a saw or knife and place your new unit onto the soil somewhere in your yard. Drill about 24 to 48 quarter-inch holes in the sides of your can to increase the air flow, or leave it as it is and have a closed-air system (see page 26: Airy or Airless?)

You can bury the bottom of your can a few inches below

the soil surface and press the loosened soil around the sides to secure it. To increase your composter's capacity, just dig deeper – about one or two feet down. Digging also creates access for nature's helpers to enter, decompose and "shrink" your materials.

Building a Bin

One easy way to build a simple, very effective compost bin is to collect four used wooden shipping pallets and tie them together. Many factories and retail outlets like home improvement centres throw away pallets after new products arrive at their stores. Stop by before the skips are emptied and reclaim the discarded pallets for use at your home. This fits nicely into the resource ethic of the four R's – reduce, reuse, recycle and restore.

After placing the four pallets upright to form your square bin, tie the four corners with rope, wire or chain. You can use a fifth pallet as a floor inside your bin to increase air flow. A used carpet or plastic sheet can later be placed over the top of the pile to reduce 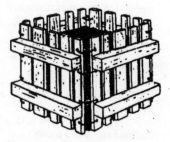 moisture loss or keep out rain or snow. If you have a large yard and lots of material to compost, setting up a second unit is a good idea. When the first unit is filled, let it simmer and start building a second pile.

Also, consider a wire bin, which can be easily assembled from fencing. Obtain an eleven-foot length of 2"x 4"x 36" welded, medium-gauge fence wire from your local hardware or building supply store. Tie the ends together to form your hoop. This bin holds just over one cubic yard when full.

Building a Compost Box

The following instructions describe how to make a moveable, wooden compost box consisting of identical interlocking sections which are stacked one on top of the other.

As the compost decreases in volume, the top sections of the box can be taken off and used to start building up a new container. Make a few extra sections and you will have a very flexible composting system.

Keep the rain out with a wooden lid or square of old carpet, polythene or hemp canvas.

The Size

The instructions given here will make a square compost box 75x75x75cm. These dimensions can be adjusted to suit your requirements and the materials available, which makes it ideal for using reclaimed timber such as floorboards and pallets. We would not recommend a box much smaller than this.

Materials and equipment

To make *one* section of the box you will require:

- 2 of 75cm wooden boards, 7.5cm wide*, minimum 1.5cm thick.
- 2 of 72cm wooden boards, 7.5cm wide*, minimum 1.5cm thick.
- 4 of 5cm x 5cm wooden corner blocks, 5.5cm long*.
- 20 of 3.6cm screws, size numer 8.
- 1 screwdriver, 1 drill and 1 saw.

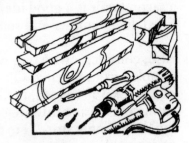

Total material for 10 sections:
- 30m of 7.5cm x 1.5cm timber; 2.2m of 5x5cm timber; 220 of 3.6cm number 8 screws.

*wider or slightly narrower boards may be used, as long as the size of the corner blocks is adjusted to suit. There is no need to keep to the same width for each section if the timber is variable. Length and thickness should be constant.

Building the Box

1. Cut 2 boards, each 75cm long.

2. Cut 2 boards, each 72cm long.

3. Cut 4 lengths of 5.5cm from the 5cm x 5cm timber. These will make the corner blocks.

4.  Take one of the 2 shorter boards and place it in position on two of the corner blocks. The ends of the board should be flush with the blocks; the blocks should be offset so that they project 2cm beyond the edge of the board, as shown in the diagram.

5. Hold the board in position on the blocks. Drill 3 holes, 3cm deep at one end of the board, through the board and into the block below. Fasten with 3 screws.

6. Repeat steps 4 and 5 at the other end of the board.

7. Now repeat steps 4-6 with the second shorter (72cm) board. for the next stage you may need someone to help hold the pieces while you fix them together.

8. Stand the 2 shorter boards (with blocks attached) on their ends, approximately 75cm apart, with the protruding ends of the blocks away from you. Place a 75cm board on top of these vertical boards to form the third side of the section. Ensure that the ends of the longer board are flush with the outer edges of the vertical boards.

9. 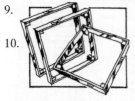 Drill and screw each end of the 75cm board, as in step 5. Use 2 screws only at this time.

10. Turn the section over so that the unfinished side is uppermost. Place the second 75cm board across between the shorter boards as before. Position squarely and drill and screw as in step 9.

You have now completed the first section of your compost box. Continue making sections until the desired number are completed.

Reproduced by kind permission of the Henry Doubleday Research Association.
© HDRA 1995. Illustrations by John Beaman.

Plastic Open-Air Bins

These bins feature air vents along the sides, encouraging an aerobic composting process.

Garden Gourmet   *Soil Saver*   *Presto Composter*

Plastic Closed-Air Bins

Closed air compost bins are the most popular models in Europe. Most are now made from recycled plastics. Many people like the idea of a nice, tidy, closed container. A closed bin retains moisture and heat. Some oxygen is introduced each time the lid is opened and through the soil at the bottom.

Some bins, like the Compost Machine, have vents in the side. Others, like the Milko Premium, also have a base plate, permanently introducing oxygen through vents at the side and also through a spike in the middle.

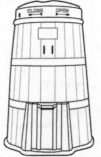

The Earth Machine   *The Compost Machine*   *Milko Premuim*

Rotating Bins

Compost tumblers are rotating units which make compost quickly. With a turn of the drum, materials inside are well mixed, and quicker breakdown occurs. Garden clippings and food scraps are placed inside a door and turned every day. To assist the process, throw in a few handfuls of finished compost, compost starter or garden soil at the start, and you will have finished compost in less than a month.

Compost Tumbler   *Kemp*

Green Cones and Wormeries

The Green Cone will digest all kitchen scraps, including some that would not normally be composted. It is not designed to make compost for removal, but simply to give an alternative to throwing food scraps in the dustbin.

Wormeries use tiger worms to help break down green matter. They are enclosed bins, usually made from plastic, and feature a tap for draining off excess moisture.

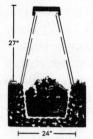

Compost The Green Cone

A Wormery

Worm Farming

Cooked foods can attract vermin. Various commercially made bins solve this problem, tumbler bins especially. However so do home-made wormeries, which are easy to make. As long as the worms don't freeze or drown they will survive. Optimum working temperature range is 13-25°C (55-77°F). You can keep worm boxes in the house, or in a warm outbuilding, over winter. Smell should not be a problem, unless you either do not have enough worms to process your material (about 2lb worms per 1lb material per day), or it is too wet – if so, strain it first.

A Home-Made Wormery

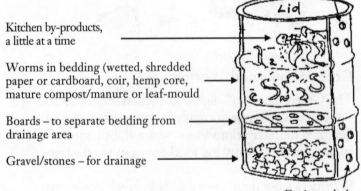

Ventilation holes

Lid

Kitchen by-products, a little at a time

Worms in bedding (wetted, shredded paper or cardboard, coir, hemp core, mature compost/manure or leaf-mould

Boards – to separate bedding from drainage area

Gravel/stones – for drainage

Drainage holes

The Great Disappearing Act

The first time you fill your bin with leaves or grass, you might wonder if the bin is too small. Don't worry, because nature's great disappearing act is about to begin. Remember that grass is about 85% water. Return to the pile in four to seven days, and inevitably it will have decreased in volume by 35 to 50% – and that's only the beginning. You can fill it again, and the same reduction in mass will occur.

4   Hot Recipes

C OMPOSTING CAN BE VIEWED a little like cooking; a good recipe will enhance the finished product. The following recipes and ratios are suggestions for combinations you can create from the materials you have available.

Compost recyclers may opt to just "Keep the Bin Full," as described on page 45, rather than follow these recipes and mixing guidelines.

The recipes below are based on volume and listed in descending order from hottest to least hot piles. A pile made up of 25 to 50% green materials, regularly moistened, will heat up rapidly and become compost faster.

COMPOST COOKBOOK

N = nitrogen	C = carbon
NN = higher nitrogen	CC = higher carbon
NNN = highest nitrogen	CCC = highest carbon

RECIPE #1

4 parts	Dry leaves	CC	Browns
4 parts	Straw or wood shavings	CCC	Browns
1 part	Manure	NNN	Greens
1 part	Grass clippings	NN	Greens
1 part	Fresh garden weeds	N	Greens
1 part	Food scraps	NN	Greens

RECIPE #2

6 parts	Dry leaves	CC	Browns
1 part	Fresh garden weeds	N	Greens
1 part	Fresh grass clippings	NN	Greens
1 part	Food scraps	NN	Greens

Recipe #3

12 parts	Dry leaves	CC	Browns
3 parts	Food scraps	NN	Greens
3 parts	Fresh grass clippings	NN	Greens

Recipe #4

6 parts	Dry leaves	CC	Browns
3 parts	Fresh grass clippings	NN	Greens

Recipe #5

6 parts	Dry grass clippings	C	Browns
3 parts	Fresh grass clippings	NN	Greens

... or your own special blend. *And always remember to add water!*

Spice Up Your Pile

The following condiments will add nutrients to your pile. These materials are not required, but can be beneficial to the process. Sprinkle the condiments throughout the pile.

Condiments

Garden soil   High in micro-organisms. Only add small amounts, as too much soil will slow the process down

Compost *   Adding about 10% of your previous heap to a new one will introduce micro- and macro-organisms (also add any materials that are only partly broken down)

Urine   Is a marvellous activator, being a free source of nitrogen and far safer and cheaper than using blood or bone.

Bone meal   The potential danger of BSE contamination is still a matter for concern.

Wood ash   High in potash / carbon. Do not use coal or coke

Crushed rock dust   Rich in minerals, feeds microbes.

* Some composting authorities like Dick Kitto mix up to 20% of their previous compost pile in with the new one.

How to Compost

Composting is like cooking, with many recipes and variations. Here is the basic approach:

1. Collect leaves, grass, garden clippings.
2. Place in a heap or bin.
3. Sprinkle with water, maintain dampness.

For quicker composting (1 – 3 months):

❦ Alternate layers to mix green and brown materials.
❦ Aerate the pile by turning and poking.
❦ Chop materials into smaller pieces and moisten.

For slower composting (3 – 6+ months):

❦ Just keep adding material to your pile or bin.
❦ Keep it moist. It's that simple!

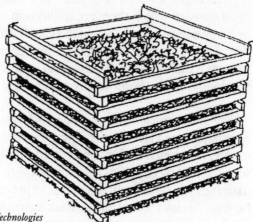

The Lime Question

There is some controversy about using lime in compost.
For the composting recycler who wants a quick fix to a
potential odour problem, a very light sprinkling may help.
Many veteran composters feel that lime is not necessary.
Using calcified seaweed adds magnesium and trace
elements too.

Compost Starter

When beginning a compost pile, you can add materials that
will increase the rate of decomposition. If you are just
starting out, try lightly sprinkling either rich garden soil or
finished compost onto the pile. Too much soil will slow the
composting process down. Soil is also useful if you are
using a drum-type system which is not in contact with the
ground.

There are hundreds of compost starters, activators and
innoculants on the market which claim to accelerate the
composting process. They may contain enzymes or
bacteria which break down fibrous materials and/or contain
high nitrogen sources. Activators add either (a) microorganisms, of which there are millions in a teaspoon of soil,
or (b) chemical nitrogen, which kills off soil bacteria, and is
therefore counter-productive. However, none of these are
required: millions of composters all over the world make
fabulous compost without any packaged starters.

There is one starter or activator which has been successfully field tested for 50 years – the Biodynamic compost
starter, developed by Dr. Ehrenfried Pfeiffer, a famous soil
scientist and biochemist. It contains a variety of plant
materials which activate the compost process in a synergis-
tic way. About 10% of all German farmers use the
Biodynamic preparations for compost making. See page 82
for more on this.

Garden Clippings

Leaves, grass, weeds, herbs and flowers are all ideal for your compost pile and will break down rapidly. When adding wet grass clippings, it helps to mix them in thoroughly to prevent odours generated by large clumps. As an alternative, consider solar drying your grass clippings on your driveway for a day or two before placing them in the compost bin; this will change them from a green to a brown material. In Chapter 7 we will cover a hot new lawn care trend: "Grasscycling."

Materials like brush and tree branches with a diameter greater than ¼" will break down very slowly. One way to accelerate the decay process is to use a common tool such as a knife, hatchet, machete, pruning shears or shovel to cut and bruise thick, woody materials. This increases surface area and allows microorganisms to do their work.

If you generate lots of thick, woody material, one option is to purchase a grinder or shredder, which range in price from around £110 to £2,000+. Shredders grind up the material into a size that's easy to compost. Alternatively, make a wildlife pile or German Mound (see p. 15).

Caution is advised in composting the following plant materials:

When adding weeds, a hot compost pile of 140-150°F (60-65⁰C) should be maintained for several days, or 120°F (49⁰C) for a longer period, to destroy the seeds. Pernicious weeds such as couch grass, ground elder, bindweed and oxalis need this cooking in a hot compost. If you are not totally confident, put them in a black plastic bag and leave the bag in the sun for several weeks. Then chop the plants up and place them in the bin. Alternatively, soak in a barrel

of water to make a liquid feed, then compost the residue (see compost tea, page 58).

Plants severely infected with insects, where eggs could be preserved or where the insects themselves may survive in lower-temperature composting, or plants diseased with rust or mildew should be handled more carefully. Temperatures of 125-135°F (52-57°C) plus will destroy the contaminants. Remember to turn the compost at least two times throughout the cycle, preferably in the initial high-temperature phase. Material on the outer edge will be mixed into the middle and receive higher temperatures, thus destroying disease or pathogens. Poisonous plants, such as oleander, hemlock and castor bean can harm soil life and should be added only in small quantities.

Ivy and succulents should be shredded or chopped up before composting, or they may regrow when the compost is used. If they do start to take root and regrow in your compost pile, pull them out, solar dry them for a few days, and then reload them onto the pile.

Fibrous plants like magnolia leaves take a long time to break down and compost better if chopped up.

Certain plants contain acids and resins toxic to other plants and soil life, such as eucalyptus, bay laurel, walnut, juniper, acacia and cypress. Having a few of these leaves in your compost pile will not harm the quality of your finished compost, but a significant percentage may deter healthy plant growth. The toxins are the plants' natural defence system, so why not mulch and put them back around the shrubs they came from, simulating the forest floor. (Research by the University of California has shown that properly composted eucalyptus leaves produce compost that plants grow well in.)

Watch out for plants that may be too acidic or that may contain substances that slow the decomposition process, such as pine needles. Special compost piles are often made of acidic materials such as pine needles and leaves. This type of compost will lower the soil's pH and stimulate acid-loving plants like strawberries, camellias, azaleas and gardenias.

Manures – A Compost Connoisseur's Best Friend

For centuries, farmers have used animal manure and bedding as soil amendments. Animal manures are high in nitrogen and are perfect for getting a compost pile cooking. Cow, goat, sheep, pig, pigeon, chicken, duck, llama and horse manure all make fine compost and can often be obtained from local sources. Avoid adding faeces from meat-eating animals, including dogs and cats, due to possible disease pathogens. These pathogens are not always killed in the heat of the compost pile. Remember to keep pets out of the pile.

Kitchen Scraps

Kitchen scraps are ideal for your compost pile. Instead of throwing away pounds and pounds of vegetable and fruit matter every week, from apple cores and banana peels to onion skins and carrot tops, you can now feed what you don't need back to the Earth.

Keep a covered bucket or food container near the kitchen sink. Put in all fruit and vegetable scraps, breads, pastas, grains, coffee grounds and tea bags. Eggshells, unless broken into smaller pieces, will take longer to break down, as will corn cobs. It's best to leave out meat, fish and bones to avoid attracting unwanted animals - use a wormery! (see p.52) By shredding foods into smaller pieces, a faster decomposition will occur. And don't forget to add wet

paper towels. The Centre for Alternative Technology recommends adding quantities of scrunched-up paper to your kitchen bucket for air and fibre. Some composters store their materials in the freezer until it's time for a trip to their compost pile. Every two or three days, take the bucket outside to your bin and dig a hole 6 – 12" below the surface. Deposit your food scraps in the hole and cover them with composting material.

Composting Toilets

The Chinese have been composting human waste for at least 4,000 years. Our 'Victorian' solution is to use clean water of drinking quality to transport excrement to sewage plants, where the water is then filtered, treated and returned - often to become drinking water again! This is obviously a massive waste of our most basic, most precious and increasingly expensive resource. Today's composting toilets (see Resource List) are a vast improvement on the earth closets of the past, and are starting to be used more - especially where providing water to a facility is a problem. The Clivus Multrum and other modern designs use a chimney to create an air flow, which means an odour-free toilet. Dry materials are added to 'soak' up excess liquid, and help maintain an aerobic environment. Double-compartment composting toilets are easily constructed. One side is used for a year; this is then sealed and left for a further year. The resulting compost is as sweet-smelling as the forest floor! Its use is best confined to non-food crops or at least crops which need to be cooked before eating, as some pathogens could survive the composting process. The spreading of uncomposted sewage sludge is being phased out, and water authorities are now conducting compost trials, co-composting with high-fibre plants like miscanthus. Woody garden materials chipped up would be an excellent, constantly available, "soak" material.

Fly Away

As a beginning composter, you may wonder if your compost bin will attract flies. Small fruit flies are often attracted to food scraps placed on the very top of a pile. Do not "dump and run" when adding food scraps. Instead, bury the scraps 6 – 12" below the surface, or cover them with leaves, straw, composting materials or garden soil. When there is no easy-to-eat food for flies, they fly away.

Careful!

In an urban setting, the question arises whether a compost pile will attract rats. The 'Green Cone' (see p. 33) has a decomposition basket that is buried in the ground, preventing potential burrowing activities. Some authorities are now offering these or wormeries to householders. Ask your Council if they provide these.

The reality is that, in most cases, rodents are more a perceived threat than an actual one. In the unlikely event that your pile does attract rats, stop adding food scraps, turn the pile, and check with your hardware store for animal repellents. As a preventive measure to avoid this, leave out meat scraps, fats and cooking oils. Sprinkling cayenne pepper liberally around the compost pile should discourage rodents if they are a problem.

Want to Add More?

Paper towels, paper towel tubes, shredded paper, cardboard packaging and wood ashes can also be added to your compost pile. It is best to recycle all the paper you can with local recycling programmes and then compost the non-recyclable and soiled papers (see Kitchen Scraps, page 41).

A Balance Between Greens and Browns

The previous recipes listed and rated materials based on their nitrogen and carbon levels. Without getting overly

technical, just remember this: no nitrogen = no heat.
A mixture of ¼ to ½ green (nitrogen) materials, and ½ to ¾
brown (carbon) materials will heat up and rapidly decompose.

Odour Away

Another concern is odour generation, which is generally
caused by having mostly "greens" and too little "browns"
or by having large clumps of greens inside a well-balanced
green and brown pile. Your solution is to generously add
brown materials such as leaves, straw, woody materials or
dry grass. Thoroughly blending your batch with a
pitchfork also helps. It's just like a soup that needs
seasoning – throw in some "browns" and stir well. Voilà –
your odour's gone.

You Can Slow It, But You Can't Stop It

If you ignore every tip and suggestion in this book, your
compost pile will still shrink and decompose over time.
With a few basic techniques, your pile will decompose
a little faster. How fast you make compost and/or the
quality of it is determined by your own personal efforts. But
no matter what you do, you cannot fail because compost
happens.

Keep the Bin Full

The composting recycler may choose to simply add materials directly onto the pile as they are generated. For busy
folks, this method works fine and compost does happen.
The organic materials will greatly shrink in volume, and
after six months to a year the bottom portion of your pile
will be rich, crumbly compost. So keep filling your bin, add
water and relax.

The layering, mixing and fast-composting methods
described in the following pages are other options for

producing great compost. They require a little more time and are appropriate for the composting connoisseur.

The Layering Method

Some composting connoisseurs prefer to gather and store organic materials over a period of time (weeks or months). When enough have been gathered, the pile is then started by placing brown materials such as leaves or woody materials on the soil as a base 3 to 6" thick. The next layer should be a green source such as manure, fresh grass clippings, weeds, herbs or food scraps, to a depth of 3 to 6".

Add water with each layer, along with any condiments. Proceed with an additional layer of brown, then green materials. This layering method is the classic "textbook approach" to composting.

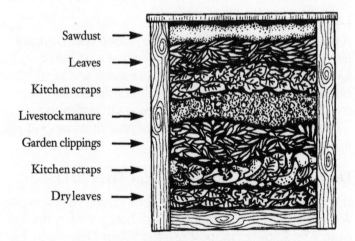

Sawdust →
Leaves →
Kitchen scraps →
Livestock manure →
Garden clippings →
Kitchen scraps →
Dry leaves →

Reproduced by permission from The Integral Urban House
by Farallones Institute, Sierra Club Books

Pockets or clumps of organic matter can form when large quantities of only leaves or only grass clippings are placed on the pile. These pockets may cause some odours. A way to prevent this is to mix materials thoroughly.

The Mixing Method

Serious composters realize that mixing materials before placing them on the pile will distribute microorganisms and balance the brown-green ratio. When materials are piled on top of each other, uneven decomposition rates can occur. For the composting recycler, this is nothing to worry about.

Start by layering materials outside of the pile or bin. Dig into the pile with a pitchfork and throw forkfuls of layered material into the compost bin. The goal is to blend dry with wet materials and brown with green materials. Once the pile has started to simmer, fresh materials may be added by incorporating them into the center of the composting material.

Lazy Composting

A popular and practical method is to locate your compost pile in a place where you plan to plant the next season. Cover it with a carpet, plastic sheet or straw and let nature's helpers do their work. After 6 to 12 months, remove the cover and plant in your now nutrient-rich garden soil. Then move to the next spot and put your next compost pile to bed.

Do You Want to Compost in Less Than 30 Days?

If you need finished compost for your garden right away or you are a Type-A fast-paced person, here are a few tips from a Sri Lankan compost master, Victor Dalpadado. He

began experimenting with composting systems while working as an agricultural extension agent in his country. He wanted to develop a composting business for Sri Lankans who had no daily jobs and foraged for their sustenance. His research identified five key points to follow in making quick compost:

1. Vary the materials, in order to provide a balanced food supply for microorganisms.

2. Mix all materials thoroughly instead of making layers.

3. Make many scratches and cuts in stems and leaves to provide entry for microorganisms.

4. Turn frequently for aeration.

5. Maintain ample moisture.

He suggests that proportions be about ⅔ brown (carbon) materials and ⅓ green (nitrogen) materials by volume. Breaking the skin of plant materials is very important to allow microorganisms to do their work. Dalpadado recommended the first turning be made on the second day after the pile is built. Turn it again on the fourth, seventh and tenth days. It should begin to cool in temperature from 140-160°F (60-71°C) to about 100°F (38°C), at which point the compost is ready to use.

To Turn or Not to Turn

Unless speed is your priority, frequent turning is not necessary. Many composters never turn their piles. The purpose of turning is to increase oxygen flow and blend materials. The following section discusses several ways to accomplish this. The next time someone says you must turn your pile over, just say, "What's the hurry?"

Let the Air Flow

There are several ways to increase oxygen in the pile. Old-time composters often place branches or old shipping pallets on the bottoms of their piles to increase the air flow within them. After the pile is built, an easy way to introduce air is to use a pitchfork, rod or compost-turning tool and poke several deep holes into the heart of the pile. Gardening stores and catalogues often sell compost-turning units that are easy to use and that work well. Another method is to completely knock down the pile and then build it again, mixing contents as you do so. Every composter has his or her own individual way which works best. The fun part of composting is discovering what works for each of us.

Don't Forget to Add Water

Now is a good time to turn back to page 13 and study the Compost Happens wheel. If the only things you remember are the elements of this wheel, you will have enough knowledge to compost successfully. Maintaining an adequate moisture level will create a friendly home for the microorganisms, earthworms and insects. The pile should be about as wet as a squeezed-out sponge. In a hot climate, a cover will retain moisture. If your compost pile does get dry, soak it and the composting process will resume. But remember that a pile that is too wet day after day will not compost properly either.

5   *Nature's Helpers*

ONE OF THE BEAUTIFUL ASPECTS OF COMPOSTING is that nature does most of the work for you. Tiny microorganisms and visible macroorganisms will break down organic matter for you. No vacation or medical benefits are required: a cost-effective public works department for the 21st century! These same organisms are even being used to break down toxic petrochemical solvents into nontoxic basic elements.

Micro-organisms

There are three groups of bacteria: psychrophiles, mesophiles and thermophiles. These micro-organisms secrete enzymes to digest the food you provide for them.

Fungi & Enzymes

These composters' helpers work together in breaking down dense materials such as cellulose and lignins inside woody matter. Three things – food (organic matter), air and water – are all that are needed to keep microorganisms alive and working in your garden 24 hours a day.

Earth Recyclers

Earthworms are great at recycling decomposing organic matter into rich humus. They generate nutrient-rich worm castings which improve soil fertility and structure.

"Earthworms increase the amount of humus (decomposed organic matter) in the soil and they are important for turning nutrients into a form available for plants," according to Matthew Werner of the University of California at Santa Cruz's Agroecology Program. Many gardening and farming practices, such as frequent tilling of

soil and the use of chemical fertilizers or pesticides, harm earthworms and their habitat.

Either It's Earthworm Food or It's Not

Before adding any materials to your garden, it's important to consider their effects on earthworm populations.

Researchers at the University of Kentucky discovered that a single application of common pesticides – benomyl, ethoprop, carbonyl or bendiocarb – at recommended label rates killed 60 – 99% of earthworms.

Lawn and garden products often contain substances which are toxic to earthworms. If it's a synthetic, oil-derived product, it's not earthworm food. Compost, mulch, seaweed, crushed rock fertilizer and green sand all feed the soil and earthworms.

The next time you consider buying a product to apply in your garden, ask yourself or the retailer, "Is this earthworm food or not?" If you don't, the Earth's greatest recyclers may leave your garden.

Buying Earthworms for Your Garden

Follow the suggestions in this chapter, and earthworms will generally find your garden. If this doesn't happen, one option is to purchase earthworms from a garden centre or mail order company.

Red worms are a productive and thus popular strain to introduce to your garden. When you receive them, make sure they have lots of organic material to eat, preferably in a cool, shaded area of your yard. The edge of a compost pile is fine, but not in the middle – it's too hot!

The Living
Compost System

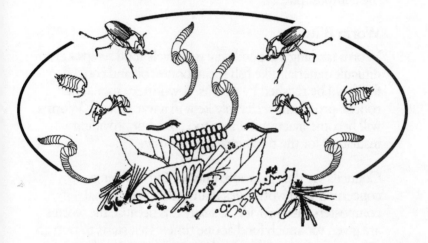

Compost Creatures

- ❧ Worms and insects work through leaves, grass, and other organic materials, creating air shafts and rich worm castings.

- ❧ Bacteria and fungi create heat as they digest these materials.

- ❧ Nature's helpers continually mix organic matter and release nutrients so that plants can absorb them again.

Last But Not Least

Let's not forget about the many other macro-organisms which play an important role in your compost pile. These are the larger creatures you can actually see. Insects, mites and nematodes are busy chewing and digesting materials in the compost pile.

Worm Bins

Worm farming is a good way to recycle food scraps - even difficult materials like fish meat, bones, oil and cooked foods wil be relished by worms. A wormery should be rodent-proof and preferably kept in a warm place. Worms will become inactive if it gets too cold, but providing insulation for the bins helps enormously.

Councils say they get more queries and problems concerned with wormeries than with conventional composters they provide. Usually it is because the worms are given too much food at one time - so it starts to putrefy - decompose anaerobically. It's smelly, wet and attracts flies. Worms must be farmed and, like all farm animals, a small amount of food regularly is best. There are a number of proprietary wormeries on the market.

If you are a flat-dweller and don't have room for a compost bin, you may still want to recycle food scraps. An indoor worm bin will produce fabulous fertilizer (earthworm castings) that plants absolutely love.

6 *Down to Earth*

COMPOSTERS REALIZE that applying rich compost generously on gardens or landscapes represents a prudent investment.

A Soil Bank Account

Adding compost to your landscape is like setting up a savings account in a bank. The interest you draw from your compost soil bank is healthier plants, reduced water and fertilizer bills, a reduction in pest problems and an inner satisfaction from thoughtful Earth stewardship.

How Composting Can Benefit Your Soil

- Compost increases organic matter in soils.

- Compost builds sound root structure.

- Compost makes clay soils airy so they drain.

- Compost gives sandy soils body to hold moisture.

- Compost attracts and feeds earthworms.

- Compost balances pH (acidity/alkalinity) of soil.

- Compost reduces water demands of plants and trees.

- Compost helps control soil erosion.

- Compost reduces plant stress from drought and freezes.

- Compost can extend the growing season.

- Compost improves vitamin and mineral content in food grown in compost-rich soils.

- Compost generously applied replaces reliance upon petrochemical fertilizers.

There are many environmental side effects from the use of petrochemical fertilizers. Their production generates and releases hazardous waste and pollution into the Earth's atmosphere, contaminates our water supplies with poisonous nitrates and perpetuates resource depletion.

Harvesting Your Compost

Your compost is ready when the materials you placed in your pile have been transformed and blended into a crumbly, humus-rich soil. The heat of the compost pile will have dissipated and the ready-to-use compost should feel like good garden soil with a sweet, clean aroma. Some composters place the finished compost into two- or three-inch-high piles for a few days, to allow any earwigs, etc., a chance to migrate back to the unfinished compost pile and continue their work.

Another idea is to start a new pile in late autumn and cover your first pile with a sheet of plastic, straw or other material. This allows the compost to season until early spring when you're ready to use it.

Once your compost is finished, you may wish to sift it to further refine your working medium. This assists the growing process of root vegetables, but it is not required. Build your own compost screen from 30" pieces of 2"x 4" timber and ⅜" metal mesh.

*Reproduced by permission
from* The Integral Urban House
by Farallones Institute, Sierra Club Books

How to Use Compost

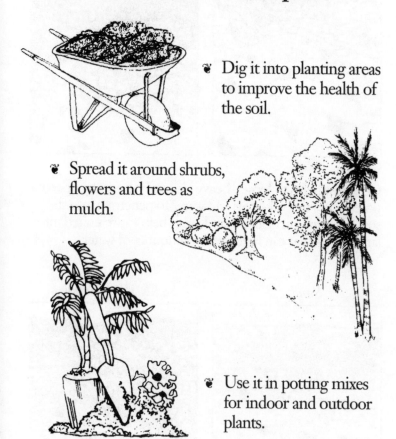

❧ Dig it into planting areas to improve the health of the soil.

❧ Spread it around shrubs, flowers and trees as mulch.

❧ Use it in potting mixes for indoor and outdoor plants.

❧ Example of a potting mix (which will vary according to strength and quality of compost):

1 part sand
2 parts loam (sterilised soil)
2 parts compost

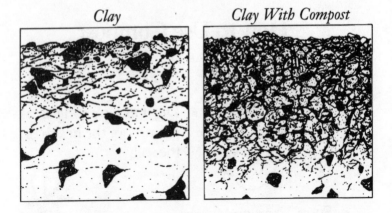

Clay   Clay With Compost

Compost helps to loosen heavy clay soil (above) by opening pore spaces that allow air and water to penetrate into the soil. The fine particles in sandy soil (below) are united into larger ones that can hold greater amounts of water.

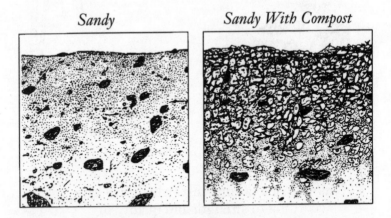

Sandy   Sandy With Compost

Reprinted from The Rodale Guide to Composting, © *1979 by Rodale Press, by Jerry Minnich, Marjorie Hunt and the editors of Organic Gardening Magazine. Permission granted by Rodale Press, Inc., Emmaus, PA 18098.*

Lawns

To build a lawn that stays green all summer with low water demand, use compost generously. In building a new lawn, work in large amounts of compost to a depth of at least 6" before planting seed or laying turf. Another method is to use a spike-toothed aerator and apply compost into the holes made by the aerator.

Otherwise, you can sift it very finely through a sieve and simply sprinkle a layer on top. In the next chapter, we will discuss the benefits of using a mulching mower and leaving grass clippings on your lawn.

Trees

Applying compost in a wide ring directly below the dripline of a tree feeds the root system. When planting tree seedlings, blend some compost with existing soil as a soil enrichment.

Applying a mulch or semi-finished compost material around the base of plants and trees reduces water requirements and protects them from freezing and drought.

Garden Beds

Add a top dressing of compost to plants, shrubs, flowers or vegetable gardens. Applying compost once or twice a year will ensure a beautiful garden and earthworms will love it. The more applications of it, the better. You can either leave the compost on the soil surface as a mulch or work it into the soil.

Good Compost Grows Good Food

Once you have produced a batch of rich compost, you may wish to plant a small, food-producing garden bed.

There is no better time to start your planting than before the spring or fall growing seasons. A wide variety of books on gardening is available at your local library or bookstore. We recommend Basil Caplan's *Complete Manual of Organic Gardening*; John Jeavon's *Growing More Vegetables*; and Bill Mollison's *Permaculture: A Practical Guide for a Sustainable Future* (see Resource List).

Tea Time

For years, gardeners and farmers have made their own brew of liquid fertilizer by placing finished compost or manure in a hessian or perforated fertilizer sack immersed in a barrel of rain-water. Nutrient-rich compost tea is ready in three days and can be poured onto plants to quickly feed them and stimulate their growth.

Research done by Eco-Sci in Exeter has proved that foliar diseases in plants have been suppressed through aerial applications of compost teas and leachates (the liquid which comes from the composting process, and can be used like compost tea). Compost tea also makes a great starter in a new pile, accelerating the decomposition process.

Another brew you can make is weed tea. Collect fresh-cut weeds (preferably before they go to seed), or roots, combine them with water and compost in a container and let it sit for 7 – 14 days. This liquid fertilizer can be blended with four parts water. Then sprinkle this tea as a fertilizer over your plants to increase their health and vitality. Don't forget you can also use this method to kill pernicious weed roots (see page 40).

Seaweed

Seaweed has been applied as a soil-enriching amendment throughout history. In 1681, a royal decree was issued in France regulating the type, location and use of seaweed (in that case, kelp for agriculture).

Seaweed contains rich quantities of minerals and valuable micronutrients like algins, which field tests show can increase plant yields and germination rates. Seaweed can either be applied as a soil amendment or sprayed as foliar feed directly onto leaves and flowers.

Rock Dust

Crushed basalt, granite and other rocks ground into a fine powder have the ability to "mineralize" the Earth's soil.[1] In Europe, there are dozens of fertilizer companies that crush and sell rock dust as a soil amendment, and experiments there with rock dust indicate that it can greatly improve the health of trees damaged by acid rain. In America, more people are becoming aware of the benefits of adding rock dust to gardens and demineralized soils. Adding it to compost piles or mixing it in with finished compost provides valuable minerals for microorganisms to feed on and convert into usable plant food over time.

Growing Your Own Fertilizer

Organic gardeners and farmers have relied for centuries on planting green cover crops which convert atmospheric nitrogen into soil-nitrogen fertilizer. When crops like clover, vetch or beans are grown and then ploughed into the soil, nitrogen levels and organic matter in the soil are boosted. The plants use solar energy to do this. Organic growers grow Russian Comfrey to make a rich, concentrated juice, full of potassium.

Health Begins in the Soil

Over the last 50 years, a major change in agriculture has occurred due to reliance on increasing amounts of petrochemicals on our farms. Half a century ago, farmers still produced nutritious food. No one needed vitamins or

[1] See *Secrets of the Soil* by Tompkins and Byrd in the Resource List.

minerals in plastic bottles, because farmers applied nutrient-rich compost to the soil, which created vitamin- and mineral-rich foods. Selenium, an important cancer- preventing mineral, was always found in fresh produce like corn. Today, it is disappearing from food grown in depleted soils where oil-based fertilizers have replaced compost.

"In my humble opinion, the farm problem is the greatest crisis facing America. It is basic and fundamental, and it should have our number one priority, for our health's sake. The farmers are our doctors. The soil nurtures us. Between the farmers and the soil, we have the combination that gives us our well-being for the future," says Bernard Jensen, Ph.D., in his book, *Vibrant Health From Your Kitchen*.

Old Seeds Sprout Again

E.E.C. seed patenting legislation has effectively outlawed the selling of many old vegetable varieties. To register a new variety costs "about £2000 in the first place, with an annual renewal fee of £350 to keep them on the [National] list if they pass." So writes Jeremy Cherfas in the introduction to the *Seed Savers Handbook* (see Resource List). No wonder so many varieties have been lost. Seed companies cannot afford to pay this price on every variety, every year, and so the more commercially favoured varieties are predominant. Commerical growers' interests are very different from the amateur's. We don't want our entire crop ready at the same moment for large-scale mechanical harvesting. We don't want tough bruise- resistant tomatoes. We want varieties that give us the longest possible cropping season - the very best flavour, different colours, shapes and textures and superior nutritive qualities. By saving and growing old seed varieties, you increase your garden's genetic diversity as well as enjoying these beneficial traits.

7 *The Green, Green Grass of Home*

FOR YEARS, people have been mowing and bagging grass clippings, and ultimately sending them to the landfill. Grass clippings are fine materials to place in your compost pile. Another option to consider is Grasscycling. Lawn care specialists, such as the Professional Lawn Care Association of America (PLCAA), recommend Grasscycling, which is the natural recycling of grass clippings by leaving them on the lawn after mowing. Manufacturers of lawn mowers now offer models called mulching mowers which finely cut up the grass blades and return them to the lawn.

Much of the following information was generously provided by *The Chemical Free Lawn: The Newest Varieties and Techniques to Grow Lush, Hardy Grass*, a book by Warren Schultz, Biological Urban Gardening Services, and the *Mulching and Backyard Composting Guide*, by the McNelly Group and PLCAA.

The Irony of the Grass Grower

"In my business, I have thousands of 'farmers' who grow a crop for me. This is a special crop that generates no revenue for the farmer, feeds no animals or people, but they fertilize and water it just the same. These farmers harvest the crop weekly and purchase expensive plastic bags to contain the harvest. Then they *pay* either the government or private companies to collect the containers and bring them to me where they pay again to have me dispose of the packages and do something to make their crop disappear! What I do with it is turn it into a soil

enhancer, screen it, put it into even more expensive plastic bags, and sell it back to these same farmers so they can produce more of the crop that they are so willing to pay to get rid of."

This storyteller, Jim McNelly, is talking about the process whereby grass clippings are bagged, collected and converted into compost in a municipal composting operation and then sold back to homeowners as organic soil enrichers.

Grasscycling Improves Lawn Quality

Grass clippings are a good source of free fertilizer and an important part of a low-maintenance fertilizer schedule. They can provide up to one-half of the nitrogen needed by a lawn. Rake them up and you're robbing your turf of food, which you will have to replace.

Golf courses Grasscycle because of the time savings and health benefits for their well-manicured turf.

Clippings Do Not Cause Thatch

In the 1960s, it was commonly believed that grass clippings were a major component of thatch, and that removing clippings would dramatically slow thatch development. In 1969, researchers at the University of Rhode Island published a detailed study of thatch, which showed that thatch was composed of grass roots.

A separate study at the University of Connecticut Agricultural Experiment Station also dispelled the fear that leaving the clippings would lead to thatch buildup. By tracing the grass clippings with isotopes, researchers found that clippings begin to decompose almost immediately. Within a

week after cutting, the nitrogen from the clippings begin to show up in new growth of grass.

Implementing an organic lawn-care program is an important component of Grasscycling. Rapid breakdown of clippings is dependent on a live and active soil system. Chemical fertilizers reduce the population of decomposers – earthworms, bacteria, fungi and other microorganisms.

Don't Bag It in Texas

In the summer of 1989, in Fort Worth, Texas, an innovative lawn-care program began. Nearly 200 volunteers signed up for the "Don't Bag It Lawn Care Plan," designed to end the bagging of grass clippings through the use of mulching lawn mowers.

Nearly all of the participants stayed with the program. The homeowners rated their lawns at 2.4 on a scale of 1 to 4 (four being excellent) prior to the program. After starting the program, they rated their lawns at 3.4, a 30% improvement. Ninety-two percent expressed satisfaction with their lawns and many noted that their lawns looked better than they had in years.

Grasscycling Saves Time and Work

This same Texas program found that homeowners who chose Grasscycling mowed 5.4 times per month, versus 4.1 times when they bagged clippings. But during six months of recycling clippings, these homeowners saved an average of seven hours of garden work because of reduced bagging time.

Grasscycling Precautions

Proper mowing is essential for Grasscycling to work successfully. Lawns must be mowed more frequently, and varying the mowing pattern is helpful. Grass must be cut when it is dry and at the proper height, without removing more than 33% of the leaf blade at one time. The only time to routinely remove clippings is when converting from a chemical system, especially if you already have a thatch problem. You can also rake up clippings after the first mowing in the spring to help the grass green up, and also after the last fall mowing to reduce the chance of disease. Finally, remove clippings whenever you cut off more than one-half of the
top growth.

Reel Cutters vs. Gas Guzzlers

Remember the old days when people used bulky, hand-pushed lawn mowers? Today, there is a new generation of easy-to-use, lightweight push mowers, as shown at right, called reel mowers. They have no engines that cause air or noise pollution.

Reel Cutters Are Low-Maintenance

No engine also means no petrol, oil or spark plugs. With reel mowers, all you need to do is sharpen the blades every other season. Petrol-powered rotary blades need to be sharpened more frequently, and a sharp blade is important for Grasscycling.

Real Demand for Reel Mowers

The largest manufacturer of reel mowers, American Lawn Mower Company/Great States Corporation, has seen demand increase significantly in recent years. Over 100,000 units are sold each year. An English advertisement from the 1830s called reel mowers "an amusing, useful, and healthy exerciser for the country gentleman."

California Gold

If you live in an arid or semi-arid region, you might be questioning the need to have a lawn that requires importing vast quantities of water from wetter bioregions far away. In Los Angeles, at a model ecological demonstration home called Eco-Home, founder Julia Russell proudly grows her California Gold lawn. During the winter and spring, the western wheat grass and fescue grows bright and green, quenched only by infrequent rains. In summer, it dies back. The lawn retains its California Gold look until the next rainfall.

8   Just Say No

IT'S HARD TO BELIEVE that our home gardens and lawns receive the heaviest application of pesticides of any productive land. But according to a 1980 report by the prestigious National Academy of Sciences, this is true.

Toxic Pesticides

People are becoming increasingly concerned about the indiscriminate use of pesticides. "It's awfully tough for the home gardener to use chemicals safely," says Eliot Roberts, Director of the Lawn Institute, a seedsmen association. "It's just asking too much. People are using pesticides and they don't know what they're doing. The result is damage to their properties and their neighbors' properties, pollution of soils and contamination of water. It's a very sorry situation."

The most commonly used herbicide in lawns is 2, 4-D. This chemical is far from safe. It is a component of the defoliant Agent Orange and contains traces of highly toxic dioxins.

The U.S. government is finally acknowledging that the widespread use of pesticides on farmland is no longer the solution. "The insects are already winning," said David R. Mackenzie, who oversees much of the U.S. Department of Agriculture's scientific research, in a *Los Angeles Times* article on June 27, 1991. "The use of pesticides is up but so is the amount of crop loss. We're losing more now than we ever have …We've pushed the traditional system to its limit, and that's where we are having our problems."

Moving Away From Synthetic Chemicals

The tide has begun to turn against chemical lawn treatment. At university and research laboratories, scientists are paying attention to low-maintenance, non-chemical techniques. Breeders are introducing new grass varieties that resist both disease and insects.

Organic Fertilizers vs. Synthetic

Legally there is no clear definition for organic fertilizers. Some chemical fertilizer companies, in an attempt to cash in on the public's interest in organic fertilizers, are simply changing the label of their chemical fertilizers. If a fertilizer contains any organic matter, the new label stresses the fact that it is an "Organic Base" fertilizer.

There are no rules or regulations as to the percentage of organic material that a fertilizer must contain to use the words Organic Base. Watch out for products labeled "organic" that contain urea, a petrochemical derivative. To obtain a totally organic fertilizer (containing no petroleum products) be sure to read the entire label and ask your retailer.

Organic farming methods do not use any petrochemical-based fertilizers, pesticides or herbicides. New research confirms that organic fertilizers are better for our lawns and gardens, and researchers are learning that common pesticides actually harm our soil. Whether starting from scratch or improving your old lawn, you can do it without chemicals.

"Natural, organic fertilizers are the best type to use because they are slow acting," says Eliot Roberts of the U.S. Lawn

Institute. "People have to mow them so much because they use extra water and extra fertilizer, which keeps them growing fast all summer. You get a slow rate of growth by using natural, organic fertilizers."

Organic Landscape Services

"We get calls on a daily basis from people all over the U.S. and Canada looking for a service that uses integrated pest management (IPM) or organic methods," says Steven M. Zien, executive director of Biological Urban Gardening Services, or BUGS, in Citrus Heights, California. These and other organic services like Natural Lawn, a nationally franchised lawn-care service, are increasing in number due to popular demand.

9 *Miracle Mulch*

I N CHAPTER 6, WE USED THE ANALOGY that applying
generous amounts of compost is like setting up a bank
account. In the case of mulch, you are purchasing an
insurance policy to ensure the health of your garden,
protecting it from scorching heat, howling winds and
pouring rains.

Mother Nature Is a Mulcher

In observing nature, we see that plants and trees drop
leaves around their bases. This assists their continued
growth. A layer of vegetative matter protects the bare
soil during the summer months by reducing the soil
temperature, weed growth and evaporation loss. Mulching
increases the population of soil organisms such as earthworms. Upon removing this magic mulch, soil life and
plants become stressed and watering requirements are
increased.

During strong winds or torrential rains, bare soil can
be blown or washed away. A covering of mulch will
prevent this from occurring.

To Mulch or to Compost ?

There are some dedicated mulchers who never even
bother with composting. They like to add thin layers
of organic matter to their garden and let nature slowly
break it down, transforming it into rich humus. Depending
on your objective, this can be a good, low-maintenance
strategy. Any one material *in quantity* can be difficult to
compost. A whole trailer-load of old thatching straw, or a
great mass of grass cuttings, for instance. But materials in
quantity can make perfect mulches. A *barrier mulch* of
newspaper and/or cardboard can be covered with a layer of

Nature Mulches in Forests

"Nature designed a forest as an experiment in unpredictability.
We are trying to design a regulated forest."

– Chris Maser, author of *The Redesigned Forest*

The way we treat the land is a result of how we think about the land.

Photo by Greg King

Head Waters Forest is an ancient Redwood grove in Northern California.

grass cuttings and then a layer of straw, thatch, hay or chippings and directly sown with a fast-growing green manure crop like mustard. Alternatively, holes can be punched through the layers and perennial crops planted; or mulch materials can be used without the barrier, especially around perennial plants, shrubs and trees. A thin layer of grass cuttings can go just about anywhere, and a late cut of grass is just the tonic for a newly-planted garlic crop. Of course if you get the grass and the straw together, you can just co-compost them.

What Do Mulchers Have to Say?

Plants for a Future, Cornwall: "Mulching for us is a labour-saving way of suppressing weeds and improving the soil structure – an excellent way of using otherwise often wasted materials."

Nicky Scott, Proper Job Co-op, Devon: "All our beds are made by laying newspaper and cardboard directly on the undug ground ['barrier mulching']. We then put 3"– 4" of compost on top. Our paths are made the same way except we mulch with chippings."

Patrick Whitefield, Permaculturist: "I've grown spuds by the digging method and I've grown spuds using mulch, and I'd never go back to digging again!"

MULCHING MATERIALS

Straw	Feathers
Hay	Hair
Seaweed	Nut shells
Fruit	Leaves
Sawdust	Shredded newspapers
Weeds	Wood chips
Compost	Vegetable scraps
Gravel	Cardboard
Cocoa shell	Plastic sheeting

Using Mulch

Mulch can be applied 3 – 6" deep on top of your soil. Remember not to bury or dig in the mulch. Just keep it on the surface. Mulching provides ideal, moist conditions for healthy microorganism and macroorganism populations. Earthworms can do the work of a rotovator for you if you give them a chance.

For further reading, we recommend *Practical Mulching* by Patrick Whitefield.

Photo: Dr. Tony Dominski

Shredded wood chips serve as mulch around strawberries at the Gildea Resource Center in Santa Barbara, California.

10 Composting in the Community

WE ARE NOW USED TO the familiar sight of mini-recycling centres in most of our small towns, to recycle paper, glass, cans and even clothing. You may even have a collection scheme operating in your area. There are a variety of schemes now operating, from voluntary-run projects to large council initiatives. The new growth area is in 'compostables'. Some authorities are collecting source-separated materials, including compostables, which go to large scale centralised composting facilities. The Department of the Environment published a White Paper in December 1995 giving composting a high priority. The new target is that 40% of domestic properties with a garden should be home composting by the year 2000. The White Paper also reiterates the well-publicised target of 25% of home waste being recycled by the year 2000 (see page 24).

As we move into a new millennium, you too can join in these new composting initiatives. You can divert 25 – 35% of your home's waste stream (or "material stream") by composting garden clippings, kitchen scraps, and paper and card that can't be recycled. In this chapter, you will learn about exciting community-based composting programmes around the world.

Catching the Wave
North Americans began to take home composting seriously in the late 1980s by purchasing and using composting bins. In fact, 23 states have banned garden clippings from landfills, and many are encouraging home, community and municipal composting of materials instead. This is starting to happen in the UK.

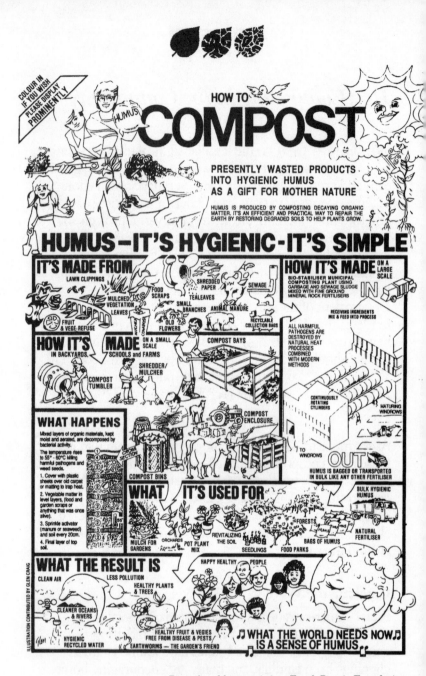

ILLUSTRATION CONTRIBUTED BY GLEN CRAIG

Reproduced by permission, Earth Repair Foundation,
P.O. Box 15, Hazelbrook, NSW 2779, Australia.

Riding the Crest of the Wave

Progressive and innovative communities realize that if they provide citizens with an easy-to-use composting unit and information, people will do their share to solve our looming garbage and ecological crisis. Surveys indicate that through home composting UK householders are already recycling over 400,000 tonnes of compostable materials every year - around 2% of all household waste. Waste analysis identifies a further 4,000,000 tonnes annually of materials which would be better composted than put into landfill sites.

Changing Attitudes

"Cutting waste demands that we change attitudes," says Lewis Herbert, in charge of waste strategy at Essex County Council. "Councils cannot hope to succeeed without educating people to take responsibility for their own waste. While home composting takes time to develop, it has clear long-term benefits compared to alternatives like kerb-side collections. Home composting will not be the answer for households on the 17th floor or for all areas. But it should be a first step for councils before, not after, decisions on extra wheeled bins for organic collections. Many councils have now circulated composting leaflets but only a relatively small number have yet invested the concentrated effort and significant resources to have a real impact."

This extends the life of limited landfills. Residents are offered composting bins which will provide them with rich compost for years, at a great price. Following the introduction of the landfill levy, it now pays councils disposing of waste to pay half the cost of home composters.

If you would like to see such a programme started in your area, let your council members and your recycling department know. Your input will help them make the

decision to start a home composting programme. A government's purpose is to serve the people it governs, and if citizens demand helpful programmes, it should respond.

Harmonious Technologies, the authors of *Backyard Composting*, have assisted over 500 cities and counties in the USA, implementing home composting bin distribution programmes. We have also published a professional 218-page spiral manual called "Keep It Off The Curb" that provides everything a recycling coordinator or citizen group needs to start up and manage a programme.

Community Gardens

People are starting community gardens in many areas. Councils have a statutory requirement to provide allotments if enough people ask for them, but in practice it may be difficult for them to find the land. Individuals often have gardens which are too large for them and are happy for the land to be used, especially if they get some produce in return. Other organisations often have land lying idle which could be used, at least in the short term. Friends of the Earth and the National Society for Allotment Gardeners should be able to help (see Resource List).

Growing food for your personal consumption is a simple and direct way to renew your connection to the Earth. Using compost as a soil enricher ensures a healthy soil. As the organic pioneers have shown us, those communities and races with healthy soils produce the healthiest people.

Community Tree-Planting Projects

As interest in composting grows in communities, finished compost can be utilized for neighborhood tree-planting projects. Compost and mulch provide accessible nutrients to growing young trees while enriching soils and reducing water demand. Tree planting projects are also a fine educational opportunity for young and old alike.

Community Composting

Community Composting is a new phenomenon sweeping the country: groups are springing up all over the place. Some, like the network in Devon, are strongly supported by the Local Authority: mobile shredders visit over 20 sites (1998 figures) when needed to help transform tough woody materials into chippings for mulch or for composting. The groups receive "recycling credits", a payment for every tonne of compost produced, which helps to fund the activity. Present legislation makes it difficult for groups to sell compost, although many do through a "compost club". This law has been challenged by the Community Composting Network and we have been assured it will be abolished soon! Some of these small scale projects have developed into other areas – growing food, working with people with special needs, or other recycling activities. There is landfill tax funding and other sources of money available to explore innovative projects based on developing the potential of this so called 'waste' material. Plants keep growing and become an endlessly renewable resource. Composting businesses give real service to the community and should be encouraged wherever practicable. Ask your Recycling Officer at County Hall whether there are any schemes in your area – and if not, why not?! Also contact the Community Composting Network (see Resource List). Let's encourage home composting as the highest priority, then community composting, and municipal composting, which is much better than landfilling, for the remainder.

Multi-Unit Composting

People who live in flats or houses with little or no gardens can also participate in composting. The city of Zurich in Switzerland has 482 community composting projects at multi-unit dwellings which range from three to 200 households each.

Zurich's experience has shown that an 8' x 10' space will suffice. Wood chips are supplied to help aerate the pile, and composting chores are shared by members of the participating households. Apartment owners benefit from their tenants' composting activities through reduced refuse collection bills. Finished compost is used for window boxes and gardens surrounding the homes. A video on Zurich's program is available from Video Active Productions of Canton, New York.

Municipal Source-Separated Composting

While garden composting is less costly and offers more ecological benefits than centralized composting, many communities are doing both. A central facility can handle commercial and residential green trimmings, grocery and restaurant food scraps, collected in specially designated "green" cans that are placed at the kerb for pickup.

Centralized composting facilities form materials into long and narrow piles called windrows. Specially designed compost turning machines, as shown on page 80, aerate and turn materials. After about a month, the volume of the piles has shrunk by 50%. Curing continues for several more months; the finished compost is then ready for use.

While centralized composting of residential garden trimmings is much better than landfilling, it requires higher operating costs for collection, processing and marketing in comparison to backyard composting. Home composting should be a part of all municipal composting or recycling programmes.

Worm Composting

Worm composting, or vermicomposting, is much less common at large composting facilities. The process relies on worms and does not generate super-high temperatures which occur in traditional windrow composting. A major

benefit of worm composting is the high concentration of worm castings in the finished compost. Worm castings are like a fine gift for plants. Plant life thrives in casting-rich soils.

Charles Darwin spent much of his life researching and writing about worms. He believed his book *Vegetable Mould and Earthworms* to be more important for humanity than his more famous work *The Origin of Species*. Ask your nursery if they carry worm casting compost. Your plants will show their appreciation with a burst of healthy growth.

Borrowing Organic Material

From an environmental perspective, centralized composting requires more petroleum for lorry trips. Organic material is being removed or borrowed from the garden for processing. By recycling – returning your garden clippings back into the soil – you continue nature's cycle of life. Remove them, and you weaken the natural system and thus waste water, energy and soil nutrients.

Mixed MSW Composting Facilities

Another approach cities may employ is to collect garbage and, instead of landfilling it, process it in a huge, indoor, mixed municipal solid waste (MSW) facility. Giant magnets pull out the metal, and some plastics and other impurities are removed by hand. The remaining materials – garden clippings, food scraps, paper and miscellaneous other discards – are treated and placed in huge piles to decompose.

The end product is a low grade of compost. Critics are concerned about contaminants from inks, batteries, plastics, industrial chemicals and other pollutants that enter the waste stream. MSW compost can be used to cap off landfill sites, or (ironically) can be landfilled – as compost it is

*The Wildcat Composter mixes and turns
the compost as it moves through the pile.*

considered inert! Mixed MSW composting was started in
Europe, where so far most plants have had difficulty in
marketing the final product. Europeans are now moving
toward source separation, with separate collection of
compostables, to produce a clean, stable and nutrient-rich
compost.

Source-separated compost can be used by farmers – even
organic ones – and horticulturalists. Farms have both the
space and equipment to make compost, and in the UK
Eco-Sci are now working with farmers, delivering them
500 tonnes of chipped-up garden clippings at a time, to
compost on-farm.

A composting and recycling society conserves natural
resources, extends the lives of our landfills, and enhances
precious air, water and topsoil, while reducing our reliance
on oil.

11 *Organic Compost Matters*

NOW THAT WE HAVE LOOKED at the ecological benefits of home composting, we can explore the important relationship of organic decomposition to regional and planetary health. The decomposition of once-living materials is a subject of importance for all who live on Earth.

On February 12, 1987, *New Scientist* magazine said, "Many of the recent outbreaks of severe erosion are clearly linked to falling levels of organic matter in the soil … the more organic matter there is in the soil, the more stable it is."

"The single most important indicator of a soil's fertility is its organic matter content," according to R.A. Simpson, author of *Farmland or Wasteland: A Time to Choose*.

According to the Worldwatch Institute, in 1990 alone the Earth's surface lost over 480 billion tons of valuable topsoil. Our soil is washed into rivers and oceans as a result of the extensive use of chemical fertilizers, deforestation and poor farming practices.

Organic Farming

Organic farming is the art of raising food and crops without the use of petrochemical pesticides, herbicides and fertilizers. It relies on the use of compost and green cover crops which supply the soil with nutrients. Through crop rotation, the encouragement of biological diversity in plants, the use of beneficial insects and protective tree shelter belts, healthy crops are raised.

The well-recognized US National Academy of Sciences has published a study titled *Alternative Agriculture* that documents the viability of organic farming, stating that the U.S. could reduce its reliance on oil and improve soil fertility and water quality. Just one example is California's largest carrot grower, Mike Yurosek and Sons. They have converted 1,800 acres to organic methods successfully. In the U.S., over 150,000 acres are now being farmed without the use of petrochemicals. Fundamental to organic, petrochemical-free farming is the building of healthy organic matter in the soil through the use of compost.

Biodynamics

The concept of Biodynamics was introduced in the 1920s in Europe by Rudolf Steiner, a respected teacher and lecturer. Steiner was approached by farmers about the future of agriculture, as they had noticed a decline in the health of their crops and livestock, and he did much to address their concerns.

Biodynamic agriculture's aim is to produce the highest quality nutrition for man and animal. This is possible by creating an ideal humus condition, the essence of fertility in living soil. Biodynamics is a scientific way of restoring and regenerating the soil's fertility.

Biodynamic compost preparations play a significant role in this unified approach to agriculture. They are made of certain medicinal herbs which have undergone a long process of fermentation in order to enrich them and enhance growth-stimulating properties. They react like yeast and dough – i.e., they speed and direct fermentation toward the desired humus-rich compost.

Biodynamics has inspired many organic growing practices. Presently in Australia, over one million acres utilize Biodynamic methods (see *Secrets of the Soil* by P. Tompkins and C. Bird). In Germany, Biodynamics is well-respected, with thousands of farms certified Biodynamic. Alan Chadwick, founder of the West Coast's popular Biodynamic/French intensive method of gardening, was greatly influenced by Steiner.

Permaculture

Permaculture (permanent agriculture) is the conscious design and maintenance of agriculturally productive ecosystems. It is the harmonious integration of landscape and people, providing their food, energy, shelter and other needs in a sustainable way.

The philosophy behind permaculture is one of working with, rather than against, nature. In the following illustrations, you can observe the important role of organic materials decomposing ... and adding vitality to the whole system. Interfere with this process and the natural system becomes weak and lifeless. One example of this would be the conversion of a heavily forested area into a soil-eroded desert landscape.

These illustrations, from *Permaculture: A Designer's Manual* (formerly called *Permaculture: A Practical Guide for a Sustainable Future*), by Australian Bill Mollison, beautifully demonstrate the dynamic tapestry of nature. The Permaculture Institute, co-founded by Mollison, offers hands-on workshops worldwide.

Agenda 21

Since the Earth Summit held in June 1992 in Rio de Janeiro, 179 nations have agreed to follow the blueprint

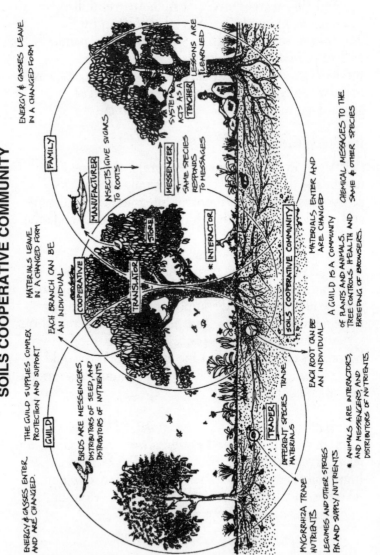

Reproduced by permission of Bill Mollison, author of Permaculture: A Practical Guide for a Sustainable Future.

EVOLUTION FROM CONTEMPORARY AGRICULTURE
TO PERMACULTURE

A. CONTEMPORARY / WESTERN AGRICULTURE   **YEAR 1**

B. TRANSITIONAL AND CONSERVATION FARMING   **YEAR 4**

C. PERMACULTURE: 70% cropland devoted to forage farming   **YEAR 8**

*Basic changes involve replacing animal forage grains with tree crops,
increasing forest cover, adopting low to no tillage on remaining croplands,
retrofitting the house for energy conservation, and producing some (if not all)
fuel on the farm.*
Reproduced by permission of Bill Mollison, author of
Permaculture: A Practical Guide for a Sustainable Future.

document *Agenda 21: An Agenda for the 21st Century*. For an easy, accessible insight into this document, we suggest you read *Rescue Mission Planet Earth: A Children's Edition of Agenda 21* - see Resource List. Agenda 21 seeks to encourage local communities to set their own agendas for what is most relevant to them. It embraces social, economic and environmental issues equally, and has already been enthusiastically taken up by many sectors of society. Permaculture designers are working alongside councils as the concerns of Agenda 21 and permaculture have so much in common. Some exciting new initiatives are appearing, among them the first publicly funded permaculture project.

Springfield Community Garden in Bradford

A seven-acre site, overlooked by tower blocks, has been transformed by residents of the Holmewood Estate, helped by Bradford City Council. A full permaculture design was prepared by Andy Langford, and it incorporates vegetable-growing, a wild food walk, water gardens and edible landscaping. There is a centre for activities, including a farmhouse kitchen to process and eat the produce. A large part of the project is educational: education in growing as well as preparing food. "More about people than techniques, Andy Langford has designed this project for the land and the community," says Chris Mackenzie Davey, Project Manager. Permaculture is far from being just a rural pursuit: it is highly relevant to urban dwellers (see *Urban Permaculture* in Resources List).

Forest Gardening

Permaculture was initially developed in Australia, and primarily addressed tropical and sub-tropical situations. On the Wenlock Edge in Shropshire, the British pioneer Robert Hart has for decades been developing his unique forest garden system (see Resource List for books and

video). In simple terms, forest gardening is based on an orchard of standard fruit trees set out on the usual recommended spacings. Between the largest trees, more fruit trees are put in, on dwarfing and semi-dwarfing root stocks. Fruit bushes are planted between the trees and all manner of edible plants cover the ground, trained up or scrambling their way up the bushes and trees. The whole system is a miniature version of a natural forest. Robert Hart claims that once the forest garden is established it is self-perpetuating, the main work being cutting back growth. Some plants are not suited to the shade created by the garden, and are grown in a clearing or adjacent to the forest.

Tree-Free Paper

Use of recycled paper is growing rapidly. However, paper from trees can be recycled only about five times before losing strength. Thus, recycling allows us to use the same tree only a few times. The "short fibres," too short to recycle back into paper, should be composted by blending them into local composting projects.

Fibre crops such as flax, hemp and kenaf make possible the production and use of tree-free paper, from which there are several environmental advantages to be gained. One acre of annually grown flax, hemp or kenaf may spare up to four acres of forest from the practice of clear-cutting. Compared to wood, fewer chemicals are required to convert low-lignin tree-free fibres to pulp. Using fewer chemicals reduces wastewater contamination. Because most plant fibres are naturally a whiter colour than wood, they require less bleaching, and, in some cases, none. Less bleaching results in less dioxin and fewer chemical byproducts being generated by the papermaking process.

Hemp has been used for thousands of years in paper, packaging, rope, clothing, cosmetics and more. In its Fall 1990 issue, *The Earth Island Journal* published an analysis of hemp's uses, titled "The Forgotten History of Hemp." In fact, as stated in *Industrial Hemp: Practical Products – Paper to Fabric to Cosmetics* by HEMPTECH, in 1942 the US government produced a film, *Hemp for Victory*, which shows farmers growing and processing hemp for fibre, to encourage other farmers to grow it for needed war supplies (for other books on hemp, see Resource List). More than 200,000 acres were harvested in the '40s!

Today, 500,000 acres of hemp are grown throughout the world. Besides England, countries that grow and use this crop include Canada, Chile, China, France, Germany, Holland, Hungary, Russia, and Switzerland. With removal of the market barriers for hemp, a wide variety of manufacturers will be able to utilize this ecological feedstock, replacing cotton, tree and petroleum-based materials.

Kenaf is a hibiscus plant annual, related to okra. It is native to East Africa, and can grow 10 – 16' in five months. The USDA considers kenaf the most promising source of fibre for tree-free newsprint. A key advantage of kenaf is that it requires 50% less ink in the printing process due to a harder surface.

Several newspapers, including the *Bakersfield Californian*, have used kenaf and are very satisfied. KP Products, Inc., of Albuquerque, NM, is producing tree-free kenaf bond paper and envelopes. The potential for kenaf to reduce our reliance on forests for paper pulp is promising.

12 *Troubleshooting*

CONCERN	POSSIBLE CAUSES	SOLUTION
ROTTEN ODOUR (anaerobic conditions)	excess moisture	turn pile, add dry, porous materials, such as leaves, sawdust, wood chips, or straw
	compaction	turn pile, or make smaller
AMMONIA ODOUR	too much green (nitrogen)	add brown (carbon) material, such as leaves, wood chips, or straw
LOW PILE TEMPERATURE	pile too small	make pile bigger or insulate sides
	insufficient moisture	add water while turning pile or cover top
	poor aeration	turn pile
	lack of greens (nitrogen)	mix in green sources such as grass clippings, manure or food scraps
	cold weather	increase pile size or insulate pile with an extra layer of material, such as straw
HIGH PILE TEMPERATURE (+ 140° F)	pile too large	reduce pile size
	insufficient ventilation	turn pile
PESTS rats insects	presence of meat or fatty food scraps	remove meat and fatty foods from pile, or cover with a layer of soil, leaves or sawdust, or use an animal-proof compost bin or wormery, or turn pile to increase temperature

Resource List

Publications

Another Kind of Garden
  Jean Pain
  distributed in the UK by
  éco-logic books

Composting the Natural Organic Way
  by Dick Kitto
  Thorsons

The Complete Manual of Organic Gardening
  edited by Basil Caplan
  Headline

Compost 1: A Guide for Local authorities, and Compost 2: A Guide for Farmers
  by Friends of the Earth
  distributed by éco-logic books

Compost
  by H.H. Koepf
  Lanthorn Press
  c/o BDAA

'Compost Box' School Starter Pack
  Federation of City Farms

Earthworms Unlimited
  by Amy Brown
  Kangaroo Press, Australia
  distributed by éco-logic books

Forest Gardening
  by Robert Hart
  Green Earth Books

A Forest Journey: The Role of Wood in the Development of Civilization
  by John Perlin
  W. W. Norton & Company

Four-Season Harvest: How to Harvest Fresh Organic Vegetables From Your Home Garden All Year Long
  by Eliot Coleman
  Chelsea Green Publishing Co.
  distrib. in UK by Green Books

Gardening without Peat
  by Graham Howell
  Friends of the Earth (UK)

Greywater Use in the Landscape
  by Robert Korick
  Edible Publications
  P.O. Box 1841
  Santa Rosa, CA 95402

The Natural Garden Book
  by Peter Harper
  Gaia Books

How to Grow More Vegetables
  by John Jeavons
  Ecology Action
  5798 Ridgewood Road
  Willits, CA 95490

How to Make a Forest Garden
  by Patrick Whitefield
  Permanent Publications

How to Make your Garden Fertile
  by Pauline Pears
  HDRA/Search Press

The Humanure Handbook
  by Joe Jenkins
  Chelsea Green Publishing
  distributed by Green Books

Industrial Hemp: Practical Products – Paper to Fabric to Cosmetics
  by HEMPTECH
  P.O. Box 1716
  Sebastopol, CA 95473, U.S.A.
  Tel 001 707 823 1999
  www.hemptech.com

Introduction to Permaculture
by Bill Mollison, with Reny Miaslay
Tagari Publications
distributed by éco-logic books

Let It Rot!
by Stu Campbell
Storey Communications, Inc.
Schoolhouse Road
RD #1 Box 105
Pownal, VT 05261, USA

Mucking In: A Guide to Community Composting
A pack produced by HDRA and the Wildlife Trust, available from the Community Composting Network (see Organisations)

Organic Gardening
by Pauline Pears and Sue Stickland
RHS/Mitchell Beazley

The Peat Alternative Manual
by Suki Price and Neil Bragg
Friends of the Earth (UK)

Permaculture: A Designer's Manual
by Bill Mollison (first published as *Permaculture: A Practical Guide for a Sustainable Future*
distributed by éco-logic books

The Permaculture Garden
by Graham Bell
Harper Collins

Practical Mulching
by Patrick Whitefield
Permanent Publications

The Redesigned Forest
by Chris Maser
R & E Miles
P.O. Box 1916
San Pedro, CA 90733
Tel 001 213 833 8856

Rescue Mission Planet Earth: A Children's edition of Agenda 21
Kingfisher Books

Rodale Book of Composting
Rodale Press

Secrets of the Soil
by P. Tompkins and C. Bird
Penguin/Arkana

Sewage Solutions
by Grant, Moodie and Weedon
Centre for Alt. Technology

Solar Gardening: Growing Vegetables Year-Round the American-Intensive Way
by Leandre Poisson and Gretchen Vogel Poisson
Chelsea Green Publishing Co.
distrib. in UK by Green Books

Urban Permaculture
by Patrick Whitefield
Permanent Publications

Vegetable Mould and Earthworms
by Charles Darwin
John Murray (published 1897)

Worms Eat My Garbage
by Mary Appelhof
(see below)

Worms Eat Our Garbage
(for schools)
by Mary Appelhof
Flower Press, USA
distributed by éco-logic books

Videos

Composting for All with Nicky Scott
Green Earth Books

Forest Gardening with Robert Hart
Green Earth Books

Permaculture in Practice video
Green Earth Books

Related Magazines

BUG (Biological Urban Gardening)
P.O. Box 206, Worcester
WR1 1YS

The Growing Heap
Magazine of the Community
Composting Network - see
below

Henry Doubleday Research Association Newsletter
see under Organisations

Permaculture Magazine
Hyden House Ltd
The Sustainability Centre
East Meon, Hants GU32 1HR
Tel 01730 823311
www.permaculture.co.uk

Soil Association Newsletters
see under Organisations

Organic Gardening Magazine
P.O. Box 29, Minehead,
Somerset TA24 6YY
Tel 01984 641212

Organisations

Biodynamic Agricultural Association
(BDAA) 35 Park Road
London NW1 6XT

British Hemp Stores
76 Colston Street
Bristol BS1 5BB
Tel 0117 929837

The Community Composting Network
67 Alexandra Road
Sheffield S2 3EE
Tel 0114 258 0483

Compost Books (second hand)
243 The Wheel
Ecclesfield, Sheffield S30 3ZA
Tel 01142 450200

The Composting Association
at the HDRA - see right

Green Books & Green Earth Books
Foxhole, Dartington, Totnes
Devon TQ9 6EB
Tel 01803 863260
greenbooks@gn.apc.org

éco-logic books / Worldly Goods
19 Maple Grove, Bath BA2 3AF
Tel 01225 484472

Federation of City Farms
The Greenhouse, Hereford
Street, Bedminster, Bristol
BS3 4NA
Tel 0117 923 1800

Friends of the Earth
26-28 Underwood Street
London N1 7JQ
Tel 0171 490 1555

Harmonious Technologies
P.O. Box 1716
Sebastopol, CA 95473, USA
Tel 001 707 823 1999
www.homecompost.com

The Henry Doubleday Research Association (HDRA)
National Centre for Organic
Gardening, Ryton-on-Dunsmore
Coventry CV8 3LG
Tel 01203 303517

National Association for Allotment Gardeners
Hunters Road, Corby
Northants NN17 1JE
Tel 01536 66576

Permanent Publications
see Permaculture magazine

The Soil Association
Bristol House, 40-56 Victoria
Street, Bristol BS1 6BY
Tel 0117 929 0661
soilassn@gn.apc.org

UK Permaculture Association
P.O. Box 1, Buckfastleigh,
Devon TQ11 0LH
Tel 01654 712188

John Roulac and the staff of Harmonious Technologies hope that BACKYARD COMPOSTING will be useful to you in your composting activities. We welcome any comments or suggestions on how to improve our book in future editions. Please let us know how your individual or community composting efforts are going. We encourage you to pass this book along and spread the composting message!

Harmonious Technologies
The Home Composting Specialists
P.O. Box 1716
Sebastopol, CA 95473, U.S.A.
www.homecompost.com

Index

Other titles available from Green Books

We publish and distribute a wide range of books and videos on practical subjects such as organic gardening, ecological building and renewable energy (and also books about our broader ecological, spiritual and cultural predicament). They include:

Composting for All with Nicky Scott video
Forest Gardening by Robert Hart
Forest Gardening with Robert Hart video
Four-Season Harvest by Eliot Coleman
The New Organic Grower by Eliot Coleman
The Organic Directory edited by Clive Litchfield
Seed to Seed by Suzanne Ashworth
Eco-Renovation by Edward Harland
The Self-Build Book by Jon Broome
& Brian Richardson
Real Goods' Solar Living Sourcebook
edited by John Schaeffer

If you would like to receive our complete catalogue, please contact us at the following address:

Green Books Ltd
Foxhole, Dartington, Totnes, Devon TQ9 6EB
Tel: (01803) 863260 Fax: (01803) 863843
www.greenbooks.co.uk greenbooks@gn.apc.org

Our books are available through high street bookshops, and also through many specialist retailers of environmental books (including the Centre for Alternative Technology Bookshop, éco-logic books and Permanent Publications - see page 92 for details).